YOUR BOOK
OF LIFE

YOUR BOOK OF LIFE

A GUIDE TO THE PURPOSE OF LIFE

JAMES MICHAEL ROCHE EWART

BANBURY PUBLISHING
Chicago, **Illinois**

YOUR BOOK OF LIFE

A GUIDE TO THE PURPOSE OF LIFE

Contact:
James Michael Roche Ewart
P. O. Box 855
Itasca, IL 60143

Printed in the United States of America.

Library of Congress Catalog Card Number:
2004112429

ISBN: 0-9706007-5-5

Banbury Publishing
Chicago, Illinois

DEDICATION

For Margie, who lived the answer
before I discovered the question.

For Mike & Josh & Michelle & Michael & Heather;
whose questions kept me searching for the answers.

For Juliette & Charlie, my parents,
who taught me the importance of understanding.

For Steve & Caroline, David & Stephanie and
their children, Jay & David & Julia & Ryan & Kevin,
who have always understood.

And for Cole & Cara, Kaitlyn & Alyssa, Megan & Lindsey,
from whom I learn each & every day.

Each life is recorded
in the Book of Life,
and in the lives
of all who share
our human experience.

Thank you, all.

This is my Book of Life.

— jmre

CONTENTS

PREFACE

The more difficult the experience,
the greater the evolution of our spirit.   — jmre

This book offered to comfort, to reassure,
to provide an understanding of our lives,
   — to find the meaning in our experience.

This presentation expands upon the central
themes of traditional human thought to produce
a reasoned explanation, relevant to the life we live.

ACKNOWLEDGEMENT

My life has been influenced by many wonderful people.
Family, friends & teachers, who offered their patience,
love, and understanding — all touched my life forever.
Although there are too many to name here, I am sure
they know that I refer to them —
                          before, during and after Arlington.

I hope to see all of you again, before I leave here.
If I do not, I'll thank you "whenever we meet..."

                          I will always remember.

                                    Love,   Jim

— Special Thanks —

To Philip Clark & Rev. Barbara Rocha
& Nancy Wallace
for their profound insight.
&
To June Rouse & Jan Miller Girando
for their expertise in the creation of this book.
&
To Gwendolyn Brooks
for her encouragement & instruction.
&
To Roger Skarr
for his excellent advice & wisdom.

INTRODUCTION

Presented here
is the central purpose of our life,
a purpose we all hold in common.
It is the reason we live our life.

It answers for each of us,
who we are, why we are here
and where we are going.

We are each here
to change the world
in our own way.

Only you can live your life.
Only you can be what you are.
Only you can do what you do.

We are each unique.
We are each part
of the infinite diversity
of all creation.

We each define ourselves
to determine the way we live.

We are more
than we know.
We are greater
than we realize.
We are more remarkable
than we imagine.

We are a reflection
of our Creator.

What we do here
is far more important
than we understand.

As we think, so we are.
As we are, so we act.
As we act, so we live.

A change in
our understanding
of ourselves,
will change our lives
and our world...

forever.

YOUR BOOK OF LIFE

CIRCLE

Life is a circle —

We begin where we end,
and we end where we began,
with the love of God.   – jmre

I am a spirit, a soul like you.
I know you and you should know me.
We share in common the purpose of life.
We have chosen to live our life,
this human experience,
to expand our spirit,
to evolve our soul
in order to better love God,
to be more like God.

We have all seen God,
been with God,
existed in God's presence.
God knows us well
and we know God.
God is not just in our future,
God is also of our past.

We have all had the experience
of God's love for us.
It is complete and unconditional.
It is the reason we have chosen
to live the human experience.

It is our desire to return God's love,
to love God as God loves us.
To be more like God
in the way we love,
that is what has brought us here.

It is the reason
we made the free choice
to leave God's presence
and to live a human life.

We are, each of us, spirits
living the human experience
for the love of God.

GOD

"La illah illa allah."

"There is no God but God."
— Mohamet, Koran, III

God is God.
God is God for everyone.
No matter who we are
or what we believe,
God is God for all of us.

God has many names
and many faces.
God will be
what we expect
God to be.
God will be
our idea of God,
different for each of us,
as we are different
from each other.

God has complete,
unconditional love
for all of us.

No matter
who we are
or what we believe,
we are all
equal before God.

We are equal
in the sight of God.
We are all equally
loved by God.

God has only one nature:
God is loving.
God's love for us is perfect.

God loves us
beyond our capacity
to receive that love.

The more loving we become,
the more we care for others,
the more we expand our spirit,
the more we evolve our soul,
the greater our capacity
to receive the love of God,
and the greater our ability
to love God in return.

God was the first to love us.
We learned to love from God.
God was the first one we loved.
God loves us more than
anyone will ever love us.

God is all things to all people.
We each will find the God we create.

God exceeds all our expectations.
God is greater that our idea of God.
God is the most profound
experience we will ever know.

God is all,
God is the source of everything.
God is man, woman and child.
God is the beginning and there is no end.
God is the Source, the Initiator.

God, the Creator, is superior to all creation.
God is the most profound existence.
As spirits, souls, we aspire to be like God.

God is more loving and caring,
more compassionate
and understanding than any of us.
God is greater than the best of us.

God cannot be defined in human terms.
God does not judge, condemn or punish.
God does not require or demand.

God loves us all,
even if we do not return that love.

God is complete unto God.

God loves, cares, understands, sympathizes
and is patient and compassionate.

God does not hate, anger, envy, judge,
condemn, punish, scorn or abandon us.

These are human emotions and human behaviors.
They are distortions of God. They are of this world.
They have nothing to do with God.

God is not concerned with what we believe,
but with how we treat others.

The best way to love God
                              — is to love others,
            to honor God
                              — is to help others,
            to worship God
                              — is to care for others.

What we do for others, we do for God.
That is the purpose of life.
That is the reason we are here:
to learn to love God by loving others.

To learn to love like God.

God is Life...
Creator of worlds,
the Source of the universe.

God is great.

CREATION

"Man was created in the image of God."
— Genesis 1:27

We began with God,
we are the idea of God,
a thought in the mind of God.

Created in an instant
from the heart of God,
each one of us
separate and unique,
distinct and different
from all other creation.

God, the Creator,
is in all creation.
There is part of God
in each of us.

After our creation
we remained with God
and received God's complete
and unconditional love.

This was our choice,
our decision,
our free will.

Being with God,
being loved by God,
and living in
the presence of God
is the most profound
experience of our existence.

It is beyond comparison,
it is beyond our comprehension,
it is all the loving moments of our life
experienced in an instant.
It is all the joy of the world
from the beginning of time,
and it is more...

It is always expanding,
always beyond
our capacity to receive it.

God loves us beyond
our understanding,
more than we will ever know.

It is the love of God.

We want to love God in return.
We want to love God
more fully and completely,
to love God as God loves,
to be like God
in the way we love God.

Unlike God,
we are limited
in our ability
to give love.

We were created
with a free will.
We make our own decisions
and we control our destiny.

That is by God's design.

LIFE

The struggle is the glory. — jmre

Before we were born,
before this life began,
we were souls, spirits,
in the presence of God.

There from God
we received complete
and unconditional love,
which caused us to want
to be like God.
To love God
the way God loves us.

For the love of God
we made the free choice
to leave God,
to live this human life,
to evolve our souls,
to expand our spirits,
to learn to love
the way God loves us.

Each of us
made the decision
of our own free will.

We are here to learn
to love God by loving others.
Each person we love
increases our capacity to love God.
With each moment,
with each experience...
                              we learn.

Each day we live,
each hour we endure,
each moment we experience,
expands our spirit,
evolves our soul.
That is the purpose of life;
that is the reason we are here;
that is the meaning of life.

Life before life.

Each life has a purpose.

We evolve through thought and emotion.

It is not what happens to us in life that's important;
it is what we become.
What we become depends upon
what we do for others along the way.

Life challenges every day; it demands our full
attention to survive.

The struggle is the glory...
              it is the life we live that is the meaning.

We are a spirit living a human life.
We are human and spirit.
Our human life is a sensory experience.
We must respond to the demands made
by our human physiology or we die.
The sensations and emotions of our human life
expand our experience and cause us to evolve.
Through our thoughts and imagination
we create ideas, recall experiences
and respond to events.
That is the experience of our spirit.

The physical and emotional experiences of life
make us more compassionate and understanding.
We have selected each moment of this life
for our own purpose.

Our life may contain tragedy, suffering and sorrow,
and will end in our death here.
Nothing we experience is beyond our ability to endure.
Our death is our return to God.

We control our reactions
to the events that occur in our lives.

If we bring forth what is within us, it will save us.
If we do not, it will destroy us.

Life is not reward and punishment; it is experience.

In life all souls evolve, all spirits expand.

Nothing remains the same.

Change, expansion,
progression are constant
in our life, in our world,
in our universe and beyond.

Our life,
this human experience,
is our decision, our plan,
our selection and our design.

Our life is our choice.
We control the moment.
We decide the present.
It is always now.

We have life
in common with
all other life.

We are all
part of Life,
together with
all living things.

God is Life.

SPIRIT

"The spirit is the true self." — Cicero, *De Republica*

"The soul of man is immortal." — Plato, *Dialogues*

We are spirits created
in the mind of God,
an idea, unique,
from all other creation;
we are life.

We live and remain
in the presence of God
together with God's other creations.
We are united by our love for God.

As spirits
we have no needs,
no requirements.
There is no time:
it is unnecessary.
It is always now.
It is always the present.

Our spirit is life,
the life within us.
It is our real self,
the animation of our soul.
It is the part of us
that is like God.

Each spirit is unique,
all are different
from each other;
yet all are connected
by our love for God.

We are all equal before God.
There is no supremacy, no superiority.
All spirits have equal status before God.
We are created from the heart of God.

As spirits living this human experience,
we are united in our purpose
to learn to love as God loves, by loving others,
to expand our spirit, to evolve our soul.

What affects one of us, affects all of us.

Atma, our spirit,
our soul is the smallest
and the greatest of all things,
except God.

We are never alone;
we are never unloved.
Our spirit companions
and angels are always with us.
They are from our family of spirits.
They are spirits, like us,
involved in the evolution of our souls.
Angels are with us to assist us
in our human experience.
We must ask them for help.
They will not intervene in our lives
without our request.

It takes great courage for a spirit, a soul,
to live this human experience, to better love God.
We are here to learn to love
and care for one another,
to love more completely.

That is what unites us;
that is the reason we are here;
That is the purpose of our life.

Our spirits, our souls cannot be harmed
by any experience in our life.
No matter what occurs during our life,
the tragedies we suffer, the pain we endure
nothing can harm our spirit, our soul.

We can only hurt ourselves.
The harm we do to others
denies our purpose in life,
diminishes our spirit
and impairs our soul.

Like God, spirits are eternal.
We are made in God's image.
We will exist as long as God loves us.

God loves forever.

LOVE

"Love God and love one another." — Jesus Christ

Each morning I rise
before the sun,
because there are
so many ways
to love you
and I need time
for each one.   – jmre

Love is forever,
it is eternal.
It will last as long
as we who love.

The more we love,
the more loving we become.

Love is the gift
of ourselves to another.

"Though I may speak
with the tongues
of men and angels,
and have not love,
I am as a sounding brass
and a tinkling cymbal."
— Paul, 1 Corinthians 13

The more we love,
the more loving we become,
and the greater our ability to love others.

The more we love,
the more we increase
our capacity to receive love
from others and from God.

Everyone we love,
we love in a different way.
We are all unique,
distinct from each other,
and all those we love,
are loved in a singular way.

The more people we love,
the more ways we learn to love;
the better we become at loving,
the more we expand our ability to love.

Love does not demand — love requests.

We each have an individual obligation
to love one another.

To love, to care for another, is a personal thing.

Loving another affects us each time we experience it.
It is different with each experience.
We are all unique.
We discover different reasons to love.
We all love each other in a different way.

Love is God: God is Love,
one and the same
and cannot be separated.

Love is care and concern for others.
Love is when we place the care
and concern for others before ourselves.

Love is compassion, sympathy and understanding.
Love is patience and kindness.
Love is support and assistance.

Love offers and does not demand.
Love accepts and does not reject.
Love respects and does not demean.

Love does not judge.
Love is tolerant,
Love understands.

Love gives and receives to both giver and receiver.
Love benefits the person loved
and the person who loves.

Love touches the heart, the spirit and the soul.
Love expands our spirit, love evolves our soul.
To love is the purpose of life,
it is the reason we are here —
to learn to love as God does
by loving each other.
To love each other is to love God.

Love is to place the needs of another before our own.
Our first thought is for those we love.

Never judge others: understand.

Make a friend of everyone.
Make the whole world your friend.

When we give to others,
we also give to ourselves.
When we give to others,
we give to ourselves and to God.

If we truly love someone, we can hate no one.

"Love your enemies."   — Luke 6:27

To love those that hate us or harm us
is very difficult for us to understand,
yet it is the greatest act of love
we can achieve in our life here.
It places our concern for another before ourselves.
We care about someone who has hurt us
and might hate us.

The injury that others do to us
can cause great pain anger and anguish.
What we suffer is very real and can hurt deeply,
yet our spirit cannot be harmed,
no matter how traumatic the experience.
Nothing we endure in this life can damage our soul.
Such acts expand our experience and understanding.

The damage is done to those
who inflict pain upon us.
By their actions, they reject their
purpose in life and diminish their spirits.
They suffer much greater harm than
the emotional and physical trauma
that we might experience.

That understanding can change our perspective
and alter our concern for ourselves
to those that torment us.

To care about them is an incredible act of love.
It is to love the way God loves.

DEATH

If I should leave before you,
I will go on ahead
and wait for you there,
and I will tell them
you are coming,
and that you are doing well.   – jmre

Death is not
the end of life,
it is a change
in our life,
it is the transition
of our spirit.

When we die,
we complete
the circle of life:
we return to
where we began...

with God.

We never lose
those we love.
They are always with us,
even after death.

Death is a change
in our relationship.
It is only a physical limitation.

We remember them,
the idea of who they were,
their persona, their personality,
the emotions that they
represented in our lives.
Those feelings we experienced
when we were with them,
are always with us.
All of that, we can recall.

Death only changes
the way we relate to them,
the way we communicate with them.

It ends our limitations.
After their death
we only have to think
and they will know and understand.

They are no longer limited
by the time and space
of this physical world.

They are able to be
with everyone they love
at the same time,
in the same instant.

They are always with you.
Think of them,
and you can feel their presence.

Remember them — those you love.
They remember you.

Death is the final
challenge of our life,
of our human experience,
that we must endure,
before we again become spirits
reunited with our family of spirits
and God.

Death is the way home.

To no longer fear death,
to see death as a transition,
a change, the return to the spirit,
that is our destination.

It is the end of our life,
the close of our human experience,
the conclusion of this human venture.
It is our return to God.

I thank all those
who helped me
with this life,
both on earth
and in heaven,
both here and beyond.

REVIEW

"Judge not, and you will not be judged." — Matt 7:1

When we die,
we leave our
human experience
and return to God.

There, reunited with God,
in the presence of God,
we will review our life.

We will relive
each moment,
each experience,
every thought,
every emotion,
every sensation
of each day
of our life.

God will comfort us
for our failures,
for the harm
we caused others.

God will share our joy,
for the kindness
and the care
we offered others.

The love we give to others,
we also give to God.

God does not judge.
God understands.

We examine our life,
we review ourselves.
It is for us to understand
our human experience.

Who better.

WORLD

This world — to leave it better for our having been here.

– jmre

God created our world,
and all the universe,
in a single thought.

God set in motion
all of the forces
that operate the cosmos,
from each atom
to each galaxy.

The world is amoral,
neither good nor evil,
as is nature, in which we reside.
The world is random,
it is a physical, sensory reality.

Our bodies are the means,
the way our spirits experience
the reality of life in this world
through physical, emotional
and mental sensations.

Each day we contend
with the moment to moment
reality of life.
We are, for this world,
a combination of human and spirit;
a balance between heaven and earth.

CHOICE

"Self is lord of self." — Dhammapada – Buddhism

We are each created
in the image of God
with understanding
and free will,
control over our destiny.

Before we were born,
before we came here,
before we began our life,
God granted our request
to live this human experience.

This life is our choice,
our selection, our decision,
our plan, by our design.
We previewed each moment
and approved each event
of our life, of this,
our human experience.

To live this life
requires great courage,
to make this choice
for the love of God.
For this
we are honored,
held in high regard
by God and all heaven.

WAY

"God has no religion." — M. K. Gandhi

There are many
ways to God.

The way to God
is within each of us.
It is between the light
and the darkness;
between the sound
and the silence.

It is different
for each of us,
as unique
as we are
from each other.

My way is not your way,
your way is not my way.
For each of us,
our way is <u>the</u> way.

From each
we can learn
and understand
our way
in a different way.

A new way to God.

God has many names.
God has many faces.

There are many ways to God.
As many ways as there are of us.
We are each unique,
distinct from each other.
We each have different ideas,
different perceptions
and different experiences.

We each must find the way for us.

We are all here for the same purpose;
to love God and to love each other.
All valid religions, theologies
and philosophies
contain this standard.

Ideas that conflict with each other,
are neither right nor wrong;
    — they are different.
They are answers for different questions
and questions for different answers.

We must each find
the questions and the answers
that help us to understand
and care for each other.

We are all here
for that same purpose,
to love God by loving others.

All ways to God
teach that,
without exception.

MEANING

"Reason is God's crowning gift to man."

— Sophocles, Antigone

This idea, this meaning,
this purpose, this reason,
provides a logical
explanation for:
who we are,
why we are here,
and where we are going.

It is a rational answer
for why we chose
to come here
and to live our lives;
for why we encounter,
what we experience.

To understand
the meaning of life,
is to give meaning
to our lives.

These ideas present this life
in a different perspective.
Understanding does not
diminish our experiences
or reduce their effect
upon our lives.

A rational explanation
and understanding of
the purpose of our lives
can help us to contend
with the tragedy, suffering,
and sorrow that occur.

Life is not about
reward and punishment.

Life is not inflicted upon us;
we were not forced to come here.
It is our free choice
without interference,
influence or coercion.

We made that decision
for the best of reasons:
for the love of God.

All that we suffer,
all that we endure,
is for that purpose,
so that we may
expand our spirits
and evolve our souls,
to learn to love each other,
so that we may love God.

We all have reasons
for living this life,
beyond our main purpose,
learning to love like God.

It may be to parent a child,
or to be the child of a parent.
It might be to touch
the life of another,
or to make a friend of someone.
It might be to save the world.
If we make enough friends
and touch enough lives,
we may save the world,
or at the very least,
make an incredible change in it.

Our lives are all connected.
What affects one of us,
affects all of us.

We all know someone,
who knows someone,
who knows someone else.

Someone knows everyone,
until we know the whole world.

HUMAN

"He that knows himself, knows God." — Mohammed

We are imperfect,
yet we can
seek perfection.

We are mortal,
yet our souls
contain our immortality.

We are human,
yet we can aspire
to be like God.

We are as humans,
imperfect in
an imperfect world.

We live life, in part,
to experience
the imperfect, the random,
the irrational, the unimaginable.

We live life, in part,
to experience
real events that
have real consequences.

Our life creates
thought and emotion.

Our thoughts and emotions
create our life.

Through life
we expand
our experience
and understanding.

Our life causes
our evolution.

PRAYER

"Prayer doesn't change God, it changes us."
— C. S. Lewis

Prayer is the act
of talking to God.

It is a thought
in our mind,
in our own words,
to God.

Think and God will know.

Prayer is talking to God.
Meditation is listening to God.
Contemplation is thinking of God.

We enhance our spirits
by prayer, meditation
and contemplation.

Pray silently,
in your own words,
in your own mind.

Simple thoughts
are the best prayers.

Meditation is a journey
of the mind through
our imagination.
It strengthens our spirit
so we can better contend
with our human experience.
It enhances and develops our spirit.
It is part of the evolution of our spirit.

Contemplation is
to consider:
God,
who we are,
why we are here,
and where we are going.

The meaning of Life.

Through prayer, meditation
and contemplation,
we reach that part of God
that is within each of us.

Prayer, meditation and contemplation
help us understand our lives,
ourselves and God.

We cannot control
the events in our life,
but we can control our reaction.

Prayer, meditation and contemplation
expand our spirit and evolve our soul.

They are our way to God.

KNOWLEDGE

"Thinking is the talking of the soul with itself." — Plato

Our life,
this human venture,
increases our knowledge
with each experience.

The more we know,
the better we understand,
the more compassion we have,
the more tolerant we become.

This is the way,
we expand our ability
to love others.
We learn from
each moment,
each experience,
during our life.

Our thoughts change,
our ideas are altered.
The more we know,
the more we understand.
We begin to view life
in a different way.

Understanding
leads to wisdom...   we evolve.

COURAGE

"We could never learn to be brave and patient,
if there were only joy in the world."
— Helen Keller

To leave
the presence of God,
to live this human life,
took great courage,
for which we are honored.

Here,
our spirit can suffer no harm,
no matter what we endure.
Even death will only
return us to God,
our ultimate destination.

We should fear
neither life nor death.
We should love
and care for others,
no matter the consequences.
It is, after all,
the purpose of our life.
The difficult part was
to choose to come here.

RETURN

"From God we come and to God we shall return."
— Koran

Our return
will close the circle.

Others we love
have gone before
and wait for us there.

We have been missed,
by our friends and
companions of our spirit,
the family of our soul,
— and God.

They wait to
welcome.

For the last time
we will cry
tears of joy,
until we find
we have no tears.

The emotion remains,
and the understanding.

But tears are human
and we are spirit,
a soul once again.

And we are home,
at last...

Home.

CONCLUSION

In closing, I offer
this final thought.

Our life here
may at times
be beyond
our understanding.
It may appear to
have no purpose.

For what we endure,
we will change
and never again
be the same.

The purpose
is in the struggle.

Our lives are
all connected.
Everything we do,
every experience,
affects us all.

Whenever we meet
after all this is done,
we will always
remember.

Remember —
that together
we have taken all
that life has offered,
and learned to
love each other.

That is what
we have shared here,
and that is what
we share each day.
It is what
unites us
for all time.

Therein lies the
meaning of our lives.

The meaning is
and has always been,
within ourselves.

AFTERWARD

For the greater part of my life, I've tried to make
sense of it all, to sort it all out, to find our place
in the universe.

This is my vision, the way I try to respond to the
uncertainties of life. These ideas are derived from
thousands of years of human thought, one idea
after another, as all human knowledge is connected.

We are each unique, each part of the infinite diversity
of creation. We all have a different perspective, we all
understand our life in our own way. It is my hope that
what I offer will help each of us to find our own vision
and to create our own ideas and that this will provide
us with a better understanding of our life, of each other
and of our entire human family.

Finally, answers very often create other questions
that require other answers. I plan to include those
ideas in my next presentation...

                              the search continues.

                                   jmre

THE AUTHOR WOULD LIKE
TO HEAR FROM YOU

The author would welcome
your questions and comments
about this book. He would be very
interested in hearing about changes in your
life and experiences that occurred as a result
of reading this book.

You can write him at:

James Michael Roche Ewart
JMRE
P.O. BOX 855
ITASCA, IL 60143

or

www.yourbookoflife.com

ABOUT THE AUTHOR

James Michael Roche Ewart and his wife, Margie, live near Chicago, where they raised five children. He served on the Arlington Youth Commission for more than 20 years and is a former member of the White House Commission on Youth.

In 1969, at age 23, he began his career as a writer and columnist for a suburban daily newspaper.

It was conversations with his late father, Charles, during the months preceding his death in 1990, that initiated the creation of this book.